BARING-GOULD'S DEVONSHIRE CHARACTERS

Five Devon Seafarers

Sabine Baring-Gould

Bossiney Books · Launceston

Contents

First published 2000 by
Bossiney Books, Langore, Launceston, Cornwall PL15 8LD
Based on *Devonshire Characters and Strange Events,* first published 1908
This edition © 2000 Bossiney Books
ISBN 1-899383-32-8
The photograph on the back cover is reproduced by kind permission
of the Royal Institution of Cornwall.
Printed in Great Britain by R Booth (Troutbeck Press), Mabe, Cornwall

Introduction

The short biographies in this book are taken from *Devonshire Characters and Strange Events* by the Reverend Sabine Baring-Gould, first published in 1908.

The author (1834-1924) was a most remarkable man. He was both squire and parson ('squarson') of Lewtrenchard, a Devon parish lying between Okehampton and Launceston. Much of his childhood was spent travelling in Europe with his parents, and he spoke five languages by the age of fifteen. He was blessed with a phenomenal energy which allowed him to pursue his many interests.

He became known as a great collector of folk-songs, as a key player in the study and preservation of the prehistoric remains on Dartmoor, and as a hymn writer: 'Through the night of doubt and sorrow' and 'Onward Christian Soldiers' are both his. And in between times, he was the architect of his own new house and fathered 14 children.

He was also a prolific writer on everything from theology to *The History of Sarawak*. His prose, like his personality, is always robust and dynamic, and his writing about Devon and Cornwall was immensely popular in his day. The present extracts will hopefully introduce him to a new audience.

In *Devonshire Characters* Baring-Gould made extensive use of printed materials from earlier centuries: we have largely modernised the antiquated spelling and punctuation which he had retained. Some small cuts have also been made, but since we are dealing with historical documents which are representative of their various periods we have not, for example, changed 'Mohammedanism' to 'Islam'.

The 'lives' in this book give us direct testimony from ordinary people of a brutal and brutalising world – one which many Devon seamen experienced with little choice in the matter.

3

James Wyatt

James Wyatt was born at Woodbury on the Exe in the year 1707. His father was a shoemaker, but James lost both him and his mother when he was very young. He had a brother and two sisters, and he was the youngest of the four. After the death of his parents his eldest sister took care of him, sent him to school, and when old enough to work got him employment on a farm, where he remained till he was fourteen years of age; but, not liking farm work, his sister apprenticed him to a woolcomber and dyer at Wembury. His master was a very honest, good-natured man, and taught him his business well, and this, as we shall see in the sequel, was of the highest advantage to him.

As soon as his time of apprenticeship was up he entered as gunner's server on board the *York* man-of-war. In 1726 he went with Sir John Jennings to Lisbon and Gibraltar. Next he served on board the *Experiment* under Captain Radish; but his taste for the sea failed for a while, and he was lured by the superior attractions of a puppet-show to engage with the proprietor, named Churchill, and to play the trumpet at his performances. During four years he travelled with the show, then tiring of dancing dolls, reverted to woolcombing and dyeing at Trowbridge. But a travelling menagerie was too much for him, and he followed that as trumpeter for four years. In 1741, he left the wild beasts and entered as trumpeter on board the *Revenge* privateer, Captain Wemble, commander, who was going on a cruise against the Spaniards. The privateer fell in with a Spanish vessel from Malaga, and gave chase. She made all the sail she could, but in four or five hours the *Revenge* came up with her. "We fir'd five times at her. She had made everything ready to fight us, but seeing the number of our hands (which were one hundred in all, though three parts of them were boys) she at length brought to. We brought the captain and mate on board our ship, and put twelve men on board theirs, one of which was the master, and our captain gave him orders to carry her into Plymouth." Of the prize money Wyatt got forty shillings. The capture did not prove to be as richly laden as had been anticipated.

We need not follow his adventures in the privateer, though they are interesting enough, and give a lively picture of the audacity of these venturers, till we come to his capture. The *Revenge* was cruising about among the Canary Islands, when a Spanish vessel ran for Teneriffe from Palma, and was at once pursued. She sped for Gomera, but unable to weather the point came to anchor within half a cable's length of the shore. She was a bark of sixty tons burthen, and as the *Revenge* drew more water and the captain feared sunken rocks, he ordered the yawl to be hoisted out and to be manned with eleven hands.

"We were three hours after we left the ship before we got within musket-shot of the bark. Our master ask'd us if we were all willing to board her. We answered, one and all, we were. We saw twelve men ashore, and made directly towards them. Our master said, 'My boys, the bark's our own, for these men belong'd to her, but have left her; let us give them one volley, and then board the bark.' We had two brass blunderbusses, mounted on swivels, in the bow of the boat. Our master stepp'd forward to one of them himself, and order'd me to the other. We had no sooner discharged the blunderbusses, but two or three hundred men came from behind the rocks. We had been so long getting to the bark that the men belonging to her, unknown to us, had got out of her, gone up country, and brought these people to their assistance. Our blunderbusses being discharged, the men from behind the rocks kept up a constant fire at us; and, at the very first fire, our master received a ball just above his right eye, and another went almost through my right shoulder. We rowed directly to the bark. The lieutenant, myself, and four more leapt into her, and those that were in the boat handed in our arms. As

5

soon as we were in the bark, the lieutenant order'd one of our men to take a pole-axe and cut the cable, saying she would drive off. I told him if the cable was cut she would certainly drive ashore, for she was then almost upon the breakers. He seem'd a little angry at what I said, though had my advice been followed, it had been better for us all; for, as soon as the cable was cut, she turn'd broadside to the sea, and in a few minutes after struck ashore against the rocks.

"By the bark's swinging round, our boat was exposed to the fire of the enemy; upon which Mr. Perry, our master-at-arms (he had been organist at Ross parish church) order'd the three men in the boat to row off. In less than a minute I saw Mr. Perry drop to the bottom of the boat, shot through the heart.

"While the Spaniards were firing at our boat, we that were in the bark kept firing at them. We fired as fast as possible, and threw all our hand-grenades ashore, which did some execution. Our lieutenant being shot, and our powder almost exhausted, we laid down our arms. As soon as the Spaniards saw this, they came on board us. The first man they saw was our lieutenant, who, although he was dead, they began to cut in a very cruel manner. The next man they came to was William Knock, whom they butcher'd in a most barbarous manner, several of them cutting him with their long hooks at once, though he cry'd out for mercy all the time. In the same manner they serv'd all in the bark but myself.

"Being in the bow of the bark, seeing their cruelty to our men, and expecting the same fate every moment, I took the blunderbuss which I had in one hand, and laid it on a pease cask, being unable to hold it high enough to fire, as the ball remain'd still in my right shoulder. When I saw them coming towards me, I rais'd it up with all my might, as though I was going to fire it at them, upon which they all ran to the other side of the bark, and from thence leapt ashore.

"At that very instant a great sea came in, and turned the bark on one side, with her keel towards the shore. This gave me an opportunity of pulling off my clothes and jumping into the water, in order to swim to my ship. As soon as they saw me they began to fire at me from every side. Five small shot lodg'd between my shoulders, three in the poll of my neck, and one ball graz'd my left shoulder; besides the ball which I had before receiv'd in my right shoulder.

"I kept on swimming till I was out of the reach of their balls; and I should have been able to have swam to our own ship, had not the Spaniards launch'd their boat and come after me. As soon as they came up to me, one of the men who stood in the bow of the boat, and had a half-pike in his hand, pointed towards me and said in the Spanish language, 'down, down, you English dog.' Then they pulled me into the boat. As I stood upright in the boat, one of the Spaniards struck me a blow on the breast with such violence, that it beat me backwards, and I fell to the bottom of the boat after which they row'd ashore. When they came ashore, they haul'd me out of the boat as though I had been a dog; which I regarded not at the time, being very weak and faint with swimming and the loss of blood. On their bringing me ashore, the enraged multitude crowded round me, and carried me a little way from the place where they had landed; they placed me against a rock to shoot me, and threatened to run me through with a half-pike if I offered to stir.

"While I was plac'd against the rock, and expecting death every moment, I saw a gentleman expostulating with the mob, and endeavouring to prevail with them to spare my life. After a small time he came directly to me and said in English, 'Countryman, don't be afraid; they want to kill you, but they shall not.' He then turn'd his back to me, stood close before me, opened his breast, and said if they shot me they should shoot him likewise."

His preserver was an Irishman, named William Ryan, who spoke Spanish fluently, and had been in the bark on his way to

Santa Cruz in Teneriffe. He was apparently a man who had lived some time in the Canaries, and had been a trader. He was very kind to James Wyatt, gave him some clothes, and washed his wounds with brandy.

After that he was taken to Gomera, where the deputy-governor lived, and by means of an interpreter Wyatt was able to explain to him that he was in great pain and had a ball in his shoulder. The deputy-governor sent for a barber, who with a razor cut across the wound this way and that till he saw the ball, which he hooked out with a bent nail. The ball had gone eight inches through the fleshy part of the shoulder and was lodged against the bone. From Gomera Wyatt was sent by boat to Teneriffe to the head governor, who received and examined him. The governor's mother took compassion on him, saw that he was well fed, and sent a proper surgeon to dress his wounds, and made him a present of three shirts and two handkerchiefs to make into a sling for his arm. Next day the kind old lady sent him a pair of silk stockings, a hat, a black silk waistcoat, and a dollar in money.

Wyatt was now transferred to the castle at Laguna, above Santa Cruz, where he found five-and-twenty English prisoners, among whom was a physician, Dr Ross. It was some time before he was healed of his wounds, but eventually did recover.

One day a man came to the castle with a drum on his back, and Wyatt at once asked him to be allowed to beat it. To this he consented, and Wyatt beat a march. Though not a skilled drummer, his performance greatly delighted the owner of the drum, and he rushed off to an acquaintance, a gentleman, to announce that among the English prisoners was the first drummer in the world.

The gentleman was much excited and sent for him, and was delighted. After that at every dinner party, entertainment, gathering, Wyatt was in requisition to rattle the drum, on which occasions he received little sums of money, which he employed in relieving the needs of his fellow prisoners.

After he had been twenty-eight days in the castle he was sent for to Santa Cruz to the general, who had heard that he drummed, and was eager to hear the performance. This pleased him so well that he asked Wyatt if he would teach the black boy of a friend of his how to handle the drum-sticks. Wyatt consented, and thus obtained much liberty, for the owner of the black boy, whom he called Don Mathias Caster, took him into his own house. As instructing the boy did not occupy the whole of Wyatt's time, he resolved on turning his knowledge of dyeing to advantage. The Spanish love black; and as the gentleman told him, black cloaks and dresses in the sun and with the dust soon turned rusty. He gave him an old kettle and lent him an outhouse, and Wyatt converted the latter into a dye-house and re-dyed the cloth garments of most of the gentlemen of Santa Cruz, and received from each a remuneration.

Dr Ross had been released from prison on condition that he set up as a physician in Santa Cruz, where the Spanish doctors were ignorant and unsuccessful. But Ross had no house to go into. He consulted Wyatt. "I will build you one of wood," said this Jack-of-all-trades. "I know something of carpentering." Accordingly he set to work, built a shanty, painted it gaily, enclosed a garden, surrounded it with a palisade, and dug the ground up for flowers and vegetables and herbs.

A Spanish gentleman was so delighted with the house of Dr Ross that he asked Wyatt to build him one. Wyatt agreed, but in the midst of the work was arrested by soldiers from Grand Canary and conveyed thither to be examined by the Inquisition, which supposed him to be a Freemason. He had happily provided himself with letters of recommendation from a number of leading men in the isle of Teneriffe to whom he had done services, and in return for blackening their suits they did their best to whiten his character. After several hearings he was discharged, but one unfortunate Englishman languished for two years in their dungeons, labouring under the suspicion of being a Freemason.

On his return to Santa Cruz, Wyatt completed the house on which he had begun, and then looked about for more work. Don Mathias Caster said to him one day, "Our hats cost us a deal of money and soon get shabby." "I know how to dye, and I know something about the hatting trade," said Wyatt promptly, "for when I was an apprentice, there was a hatter next door, and I kept my eyes open and watched his proceedings."

Accordingly Don Mathias gave him one of his old hats to dress. Wyatt immediately had a hat-block made, dyed the hat, cleaned the lace, and carried it to the Don the same day.

"When I show'd it to him, he was surpriz'd to see how well I had made it look. He told me, if I would do other gentlemen's hats as well as I had done his, I might get an estate in a few years, and that he would help me to business enough." That same evening in came two hats, next morning five – and then they rained on him, and he charged half a dollar for renovating each. He had soon realized £20.

One night he was roused by the cry of fire, and running out saw a crowd standing gaping at the house of the Portuguese consul that was on fire in the top story. No one did anything – there was no one to take the lead, and the family was fast asleep within. Wyatt got a crowbar and an axe, broke down the door, and rescued the consul and his wife and all the family save one child that was burnt. The fire rapidly spread, as the houses were of wood, to the next house belonging to the French consul. He and his were rescued. The next, but not adjoining, house was that of the general. But what intervened made its destruction probable, for this was a cellar full of brandy and rum casks. The general's house had a flat roof. Wyatt organized a chain of water carriers, and standing on the roof poured water incessantly over the side of the house licked by the flames, and this he continued to do till the fire burnt itself out.

Next day the general sent for him, thanked him for having saved his house, and presented him with a passport authorizing him to carry on his trade and travel freely between the seven islands.

In the beginning of June, 1742, an English vessel was brought into harbour, the *Young Neptune*, Captain Winter, that had been captured by a Spanish privateer. Wyatt soon became intimate with the captain and his mate, and after a while they confided to him a plan they had discussed of escaping to Madeira, whence they could easily obtain a passage to England or Holland. The scheme was that he, Winter, the captain, Burroughs, the mate, and four other Englishmen should steal a boat from a galleon laid up in the bay and make their escape in the night. Wyatt eagerly agreed to be one of the party; and the plan was carried into effect on the 29th of June. There were seven in the boat, the captain and mate aforenamed, Smith, Swanwick, Larder, Newell, and Wyatt. The boat had five oars and a sprit-sail. The captain had a compass, but no quadrant. At first the wind blew fair, but speedily turned contrary to the direction desired, so that all hopes of making Madeira had to be abandoned. The wind rose to a gale and the men were worn out with bailing. They had to clear the boat of water with two pails and their hats. On 2 July they sighted a point of land which they took to be Cape Bojadore, and they steered south in hopes of reaching Gambia. On 7 July they saw a low sandy island, and a sloop ashore, and made at once for land. On disembarking they were surrounded by a swarm of Moors, who could speak a little Portuguese, and two of them spoke broken English. Wyatt and the rest were conducted inland to where there was a village of squalid huts. Here they were given some fish and a little water. They speedily discovered that the Moors had no intention of letting them go to Gambia, but purposed making off with their boat and leaving them to perish on the island where there was no water, all that was used having to be brought in skins from the mainland.

Presently a number of the Moors departed in the boat of the Europeans, leaving behind only one large boat that was rotten, and a small one; and some of the Moors remained to see that the English carpenter repaired the decayed vessel, intending when that was done to leave the Europeans behind. These consulted and resolved on getting possession of the little boat and escaping in it. As a precaution they contrived to get hold of the fishing spears of the Moors, so that these might have as few weapons as possible, should it come to a fight.

The carpenter then, with the tools that had been given to him for the purpose of repairing the large boat, set to work to knock holes in her bottom, so that she might not be used in pursuit.

Then the little party, having got together, made for the small boat. "I had got the hammer and the adze, the carpenter had the hatchet, and the rest of our people had fishing spears. The Moors, perceiving us make towards the boat, ran between that and us, in order to prevent our getting into her. This began the fight, for the carpenter beat Marta into the water, which was about three feet deep, with the hatchet, and Duckamar presently after him. I struck Mahomet with the adze, and took off a piece of flesh and part of his ear. In an instant every one was out of their huts, and pulling them down in order to get sticks to fight us. Seeing this, we ran to the assistance of our countrymen as fast as we could, leaving the two Moors that fell into the water for dead.

"The Moors came very near us with the sticks they pulled out of their huts, and threw them at us, one of which hit Robert Larder and broke his thumb. One of our men, looking round, saw the two Moors who we thought were dead standing up against the side of the boat. Upon his saying they were there, I ran towards them, having still the hammer in one hand and the adze in the other. When they saw me coming, they ran round the boat, got to their companions, and fought as well as though they had not been hurt.

"We were obliged to keep our ground, for fear some of the Moors should get into the little boat, in which we intended to make our escape, and which was not an hundred yards behind us. At length one of the Moors came running behind Mr Burroughs, and gave him a terrible blow on the head with a stick. Mr Burroughs immediately turned round and struck at him, but missed him. The man ran directly up the island; and Mr Burroughs, in the hurry not thinking of the consequence, ran after him. We kept calling to him to come back to us, when, on a sudden, the Moors took to their heels and ran after him. Some of them presently came up with him, knocked him down with their sticks, and cut his throat from ear to ear. Some of them then turned back and made towards their little boat, thinking to have got her off in order to prevent our escape. As soon as we saw that, we all ran as fast as possible to secure the boat. As I was the nearest to the boat I got soonest to her; but there was one of the Moors had got to the boat before me, and was getting up her side. I gave him a blow on his back with the hammer; upon which he let go his hold and fell into the water. As he was falling I hit him another blow on the head; upon which he fell under the boat, and rose on the other side.

"While we were in the fight, three of our men got into the boat, and kept calling to the rest to come in likewise; which at length we did, retreating all the way with our faces towards the Moors. When we came to the boat, the other three, with the fishing spears, kept off the Moors till we got in, cut the grappling loose, and drove away with the tide."

It was not possible to get far in this little boat, and the party made for the mainland, where they were at once set upon by other Moors, who stripped them of their shirts, and held them prisoners till those from the island arrived, and these latter fell on them and beat and trampled on them unmercifully, and would have cut their throats had not the mainland Moors restrained them by saying that the King or Sultan of the Gum

13

Coast must be informed that there were European prisoners there, and that he would decide what was to be done with them. They were then tied in pairs back to back and carried back to the island, where they were cast on the floor of a tent, and left thus without food or water for four days. After that they were sparingly fed, untied, and made to work as slaves. After some weeks an officer called Abede arrived with nineteen men, reviewed them, and left. As soon as he was gone Swanwick, the carpenter, was taken away by the island Moors, and no tidings of what became of him ever reached the rest. Sixteen days after the officer had left he returned with orders from the King or Sultan that all who remained of the prisoners were to be transferred to the mainland and conducted across the desert to the French factory at Senegal, where he hoped to receive pay from the French for surrendering them.

The party had been taken prisoners by the Moors on 7 July, 1742, and they were not released and committed to the charge of Abede till 13 November, so that they had remained in durance and in miserable condition for four months and six days. At one time, when deprived of their shirts and exposed to the sun, their faces and bodies were so blistered that they were unable to recognize each other, save by their voices. They had now a long and painful journey over the desert, under the charge of Abede, that lasted till 23 December, when they were near Senegal, and Abede dispatched a messenger to the French factors to announce that the European prisoners were at hand, and to bargain for a sum to be paid for their release. They had been tramping over burning sands, insufficiently fed, for forty days. Whilst waiting for news from the factory the Moors killed an ox, and gave the head and guts to the English prisoners. They boiled the meat on the sand and devoured it greedily – it was the first flesh they had tasted for upwards of six months.

"Sometime after we got some caravances. Having eaten no pulse for several months, we hardly knew when we had enough.

But we suffered severely for it, for we were presently afterwards taken extremely ill. The Moors seeing we were very bad, gave us the urine of goats to drink. This purged us prodigiously, and we remained ill for several hours; but, when it had worked off, we grew speedily well."

Five days more elapsed before an answer arrived from the factory. On 28 December the messenger returned in a sloop sent from the factory to bring the prisoners to Senegal. The captain brought clothes for them, and gave them "an elegant entertainment, consisting of fowls, fresh meat, etc."

On 29 December they were conveyed to the factory at Senegal, and were most kindly received by the French, and they remained there for a month all but a day; and then were sent in a French sloop to Gambia, on 28 January, 1743, which they reached on 31 January. Gambia was an English settlement, a fort, and a factory; and there also the poor fellows were kindly and hospitably entertained, provided with money and all they required.

The time of their sufferings was now over.

"The 1st February I went on board the *Robert*, Captain Dent, commander, lying in Gambia River. He was hir'd by the African Company and was laden with gum arabic, elephants' teeth, bees-wax, etc. I told him our case, and that I wanted to come to England; upon which he kindly promised me, or all of us, if we were so disposed, our passage to England gratis, provided we would work our way home. Captain Winter, however, had business to transact in Jamaica, and preferred to wait till a vessel would take him thither; two of the men remained at Gambia, and the rest, saying that they had no homes or friends in England, preferred to go to the West Indies and earn some money before they returned to the right and tight little island.

"It was an unfortunate decision of Captain Winter. He and Larder sailed in a schooner bound for Jamaica, but never reached his destination, as the vessel was lost, and every one of the crew and passengers was drowned.

"We set sail from Gambia the 3rd of February, 1743, and arrived in the river Thames on the 16th of April following; so that we were just two months and thirteen days in our passage to England."

On 29 May, 1741, James Wyatt had entered as trumpeter on board the *Revenge,* privateer, and was away on her almost two years, during which time he had undergone as many hardships as ever man did – enough to break down the health of one who did not possess a constitution of iron.

Wyatt now visited his friends, and was warmly welcomed, and all would have given him money to start him in some business. One gentleman offered to advance him a thousand pounds; but he declined these generous offers. The French at Senegal and the English at Gambia had been so liberal that he had enough for his purpose. He now bought an electrical machine, and turned showman in London, giving people shocks at a shilling a head. This answered for a while, and then public interest in the machine slackened there, so he toured in the country.

"At some towns I scarce took money enough to bear my expenses, the people not knowing the meaning of the word Electricity; nor would they give the price I usually got in London; for, talking of a shilling each person, frightened them out of their wits. In some towns in Kent I had very good business, and saved a pretty deal of money; but, even then, I was forced to lower my price. In these towns the people knew what it meant, and that the thing was very curious and surprising. They came, when the price was not so high, in great numbers, and sometimes many miles, to be electrified."

He remained in Kent two months and made £12. Then it occurred to him that he would go with his battery to Jamaica, where the novelty of the machine was certain to create a stir.

Whilst preparing for the voyage, he undertook to manufacture an optical contrivance for a gentleman, and was well paid for it.

Then he bought a pair of gloves and abundance of clothes, as clothes he learned were very dear in the West Indies.

"At length the time of the ship's sailing being near at hand, I settled my affairs, took my leave of my friends, and went on board the ship on the 25th April, 1747.

"After having experienced various vicissitudes of fortune, I am once more going into a strange land: for, though there is nothing new under the sun, yet the eye is never satisfied with seeing."

Wyatt had committed his adventures to paper before starting, and had disposed of the manuscript to a publisher. The book sold well, and the sixth edition was called for in 1755, but in it no further particulars are given of Wyatt, so that it must be assumed either that he was then dead or that he was still abroad.

What strikes one in reading his memoirs is the indefatigable energy and the resourcefulness of the man. He could turn his hand to anything. He kept his eyes open, and was ever eager to acquire information.

His *Life and Surprising Adventures* has his portrait in copper plate prefixed to it. He wears a wig, and a laced and embroidered waistcoat, open at the breast to display his fine frilled shirt.

Robert Lyde
& the 'Friend's Adventure'

"*A true and Exact Account of the Retaking a ship, called the Friend's Adventure of Topsham, from the French; after She had been taken six days, and they were upon the Coasts of France with it four days. When one Englishman and a Boy set upon seven Frenchmen, killed two of them, took the other Five prisoners, and brought the said Ship and them safe to England. Their Majesties' Customs of the said Ship amounted to £1000 and upwards. Performed and written by Robert Lyde, Mate of the same ship.*" London, 1693.

In February, 1689, Robert Lyde, of Topsham, shipped on board a pink of the same port, eighty tons, Isaac Stoneham Master, bound for Virginia, and on 18 May following arrived there, took in a lading, and set sail in company with a hundred merchantmen for home under convoy of two men-of-war.

A fortnight after, storms separated the Topsham boat from the convoy, so that she had to make the best of her way home alone, and on 19 October came up with two Plymouth vessels of the fleet about forty leagues west of Scilly, the wind easterly. On the 21st the crew saw four other ships to leeward which they took to be some of their consorts, but which proved to be French privateers. They managed to escape them, but were captured by a privateer of St Malo, of twenty-two guns and over a hundred men, on 24 October, and were taken to St Malo as prisoners, where they were detained and treated with gross inhumanity, during seventeen days. Lyde says: "If we had been taken by Turks, we could not have been used worse. For bread we had 6 lb. and one cheek of a bullock for every 25 men for a day; and it fell out that he that had half a bullock's eye for his lot, had the greatest share." After seventeen days they were all removed to Dinan, where were many other English prisoners confined in the cramped tower of the fortification that is still standing, with its small cells. Here they were herded together in a place not fit to contain one quarter of the number, and there they were retained for three months and ten days. "Our allowance was 3lb. of old cow-beef without any salt to flavour it, for seven men a day; but I think we had 2 lb. of bread for each man, but it was so bad that dogs would not eat it, neither could we eat but very little, and that that we did eat did us more hurt than good, for 'twas more orts [scraps] than bread, so we gave some of it to the hogs, and made pillows of the rest to lay our heads on, for they allowed us fresh straw but once every five weeks, so that we bred such swarms of lice in our rags that one man had a great hole eaten through his throat by them, which was not perceived till after his death, and I myself was so weak that it was 14 weeks after my releasement before I recovered any tolerable strength in me.

"They plundered us of our clothes when we were taken, and some of us that had money purchased rugs to cover our rags by day, and keep us warm by night; but upon our return home from France, the Deputy Governor of Dinan was so cruel as to order our said rugs to be taken from us, and stayed himself and saw it performed; and when some of our fellow prisoners lay a dying they inhumanly stript off some of their cloaths, three or four days before they were quite dead. These and other barbarities made so great an impression upon me, as that I did then resolve never to go a prisoner there again, and this resolution I did ever after continue in and by the assistance of God always will."

Lyde returned to his home at Topsham, an exchange of prisoners having been effected, but not till four hundred out of the six hundred English prisoners crowded into the dungeons at Dinan had perished of disease and starvation.

In his Preface, Lyde says: "I here present you with a token of God Almighty's goodness in relieving me from the barbarity, inhumanity and most cruel slavery of the Most Christian Turk of France, whose delight it was to make his own subjects slaves, and his chief study to put prisoners of war to the most tedious and cruel lingering death of hunger and cold, as I have been experimentally (to my own damage both felt and seen), by a five months' confinement in this country."

Shortly after his return to Topsham Lyde shipped as mate of a vessel, the *Friend's Adventure*, eighty tons, bound for Oporto, and sailed on 30 September, 1691. Oporto was reached in safety, but on the way back, off Cape Finisterre, the vessel was taken by a French privateer. Resistance had been impossible, at all events must have been unavailing, but before surrendering Lyde concealed a blunderbuss and ammunition between decks among the pipes of wine. When the *Friend's Adventure* was boarded the lieutenant ordered Lyde and a boy to remain on her, and the Master, four men, and another boy were conveyed on board the privateer. Seven Frenchmen were left on the *Friend's Adventure* to navigate her and take her to St Malo. This done, the privateer departed. Lyde was determined not to go through his former experiences as a prisoner in France, and he endeavoured to induce the boy to assist him against the French crew, but the lad was timorous, thought such an attempt as Lyde promised must fail, and repeatedly refused to take any part in it.

After a few days they approached St Malo, and the repugnance in Lyde's mind against renewing his experiences there and at Dinan became overmastering.

"At 8 in the morning all the Frenchmen sat round the cabin's table at breakfast, and they call'd me to eat with them, and accordingly I accepted, but the sight of the Frenchmen did immediately take away my stomach, and made me sweat as if I had been in a stove, and was ready to faint with eagerness to encounter them. Which the Master perceiving, and seeing me in that condition, asked me (in French) if I were sick, and I answered yes. But could stay no longer in sight of them, and so went immediately down between decks to the boy and did earnestly intreat him to go presently with me into the cabin, and to stand behind me, and I would kill and command all the rest presently. For now I told him was the best time for me to attack them, while they were round the table, and knock down but one man in case two laid hold upon me, and it may be never the like opportunity again. After many importunities, the boy asked me after what manner I intended to encounter them; I told him I would take the crow of iron and hold it in the middle with both hands, and I would go into the cabin and knock down him that stood at the end of the table on my right hand, and stick the point of the crow into him that sat at the end of the table, on my left hand, and then for the other five that sat behind the table. But still he not consenting, I had second thoughts of undertaking it without him, but the cabin was so low that I could not stand upright in it by a foot, which made me at that time desist.

"By this time they had eat their breakfast, and went out upon deck; then I told the boy with much trouble, we had lost a grave opportunity, for by this time I had had the ship under my command. Nay, says the boy, I rather believe that by this time you and I should have both been killed."

Lyde then, to stimulate the slack fellow to action, recounted the miseries to which he would be subjected in prison in France.

"In a little time after they had been upon deck, they separated from each other, viz. the Master lay down in his cabin and two of the men lay down in the great cabin and one in a cabin between decks, and another sat down upon a low stool by the helm, to look after the glass, to call the pumps, and the other two men walked upon the decks. Then, hoping I should prevail with the boy to stand by me, I immediately applied myself to prayer, desiring God to pardon my sins, and I prayed also for my enemies who should happen to die by my hands. And then I endeavoured again to persuade the boy – but could not prevail with him to consent.

21

"Then the glass was out, it being half after eight, and the two men that were upon deck went to pump out the water. Then I also went upon deck again, to see whether the wind and weather were like to favour my enterprize, and casting my eyes to windward, I liked the weather, and hop'd the wind would stand. And then immediately went down to the boy, and beg'd of him again to stand by me, while two of the men were at the pumps (for they pumpt on the starboard side, and the steerage door open on the starboard side, so that they could not see me going aft to them in the cabin). But I could by no persuasions prevail with the boy, so that by this time the men had done pumping; whereupon losing this opportunity caused me again to be a little angry with the boy."

Again Lyde warned the lad of the horrors before him if taken a prisoner to St Malo. The boy replied that rather than endure such distresses he would turn Papist, and volunteer on board a French privateer. This roused Lyde's wrath, and he said some very strong things. He told him that this would not help him; some of the English prisoners of war with himself had turned Papists, but had already become so attenuated by disease and suffering that they had died.

"The boy asked what I would have him do? I told him to knock down that man at the helm, and I will kill and command all the rest. Saith the boy, 'If you be sure to overcome them, how many do you count to kill?' I answered that I intended to kill three of them. Then the boy replied, 'Why three and no more?' I answered that I would kill three for three of our men that died in prison when I was there. And if it should please God that I should get home safe I would if I could go in a man-of-war or fireship, and endeavour to revenge on the enemy for the death of those 400 men that died in the same prison of Dinan. But the boy said four alive would be too many for us.

"I then replied that I would kill but three, but I would break the legs and the arms of the rest if they won't take quarter and be quiet without it."

After a long discussion and much inquiry, the boy was finally induced to give a reluctant consent to help. The attempt was to be made that day. "At 9 in the morning the two men upon deck were pumping; then I turned out from the sail, where the boy and I then lay'd, and pull'd off my coat that I might be the more nimble in the action. I went up the gunroom scuttle into the steerage, to see what position they were in, and was satisfied therein. Then the boy coming to me, I leapt up the gunroom scuttle, and said, 'Lord be with us!' and I told the boy that the drive bolt was by the scuttle, in the steerage; and then I went softly aft into the cabin, and put my back against the bulkhead and took the jam can, and held it with both my hands in the middle part, and put my legs abroad to shorten myself, because the cabin was very low. But he that lay nighest to me, hearing me, opened his eyes, and perceiving my intent, endeavoured to rise, to make resistance; but I prevented him by a blow upon his forehead, which mortally wounded him, and the other man which lay with his back to the dying man's side, hearing the blow, turned about and faced me, and as he was rising with his left elbow, very fiercely endeavouring to come against me, I struck at him, and he let himself fall from his left arm, and held his arm for a guard, whereby did keep off a great part of the blow, but still his head received a great part of the blow.

"The Master lying in the cabin on my right hand, hearing the two blows, rose and sate in the cabin and called me bad names; but I having my eyes every way, I push't at his ear with the claws of the crow, but he, falling back for fear thereof, it seemed afterwards that I struck the claws of the crow into his cheek, which blow made him lie still as if he had been dead; and while I struck at the Master, the fellow that fended off the blow with his arm, rose upon his legs, and running towards me, with his head low, to ram his head against my breast to overset me, but I pushed the point at his head. It struck it an inch and a half into his fore-

23

head, and as he was falling down, I took hold of him by the back, and turn'd him into the steerage.

"I heard the boy strike the man at the helm two blows, after I had knock'd down the first man, which two blows made him lie very still, and as soon as I turn'd the man out of the cabin, I struck one more blow at him that I struck first and burst his head, so that his blood and brains ran out upon the deck.

"The Master all the while did not stir, which made me conclude that I had struck him under the ear, and had killed him with the blow.

"Then I went out to attack the two men that were at the pump, where they continued pumping, without hearing or knowing what I had done; and as I was going to them, I saw that man that I had turn'd into the steerage crawling out upon his hands and knees upon the deck, beating his hands upon the deck, to make a noise, that the men at the pump might hear, for he could not cry out, nor speak. and when they heard him, and seeing his blood running out of his forehead, they came running aft to me, grinding their teeth; but I met them as they came within the steerage door, and struck at them, but the steerage being not above 4ft high, I could not have a full blow at them, whereupon they fended off the blow, and took hold of the crow with both their hands close to mine, striving to haul it from me. Then the boy might have knock't them down with much ease, while they were contending with me, but that his heart failed him, so that he stood like a stake at a distance on their left side, and 2 foots length off, the crow being behind their hands. I called to the boy to take hold of it, and bawl as they did, and I would let go all at once, which the boy accordingly doing, I pushed the crow towards them, and let it go, and was taking out my knife to traverse amongst them, but they seeing me put my right hand into my pocket, fearing what would follow, they both let go of the crow to the boy, and took hold of my right arm with both their hands.

24

"The Master, that I thought I had killed in his cabin, coming to himself, and hearing they had hold of me, came out of his cabin, and also took hold of me with both his hands about my middle. Then one of the men that had hold of my right arm let go, and put his back to my breast, and took hold of my left hand and arm, and held it close to his breast, and the Master let go from my middle, and took hold of my right arm, and he with the other that had hold of my right arm did strive to get me off my legs; but knowing that I should not be long in one piece if they got me down, I put my right foot against the ship's side, on the deck, for a support, and with the assistance of God, I kept my feet, when they three and one more did strive to throw me down, for the man at the helm that the boy knocked down rose up and put his hands about my middle and strove to haul me down. The boy seeing that man rise and take hold of me, cried out, fearing then that I should be overcome of them, but did not come to help me, nor did not strike one blow at any of them neither all the time.

"When I heard the boy cry out, I said, 'Do you cry, you villain, now I am in such a condition! Come quickly, and knock this man on the head that hath hold of my left arm.'

"The boy perceiving that my heart did not fail me, took some courage from thence, and endeavoured to give that man a blow on the head, with the drive-bolt, but struck so faintly that he mist his blow, which greatly enraged me against him.

"I, feeling the Frenchman that held about my middle hang very heavy, I said to the boy, 'Do you miss your blow, and I in such a condition? Go round the binkle and knock down that man that hangeth upon my back,' which was the same man the boy knock't down at the helm. So the boy did strike him one blow upon the head, which made him fall, but he rose up again immediately, but being uncapable of making any further resistance, he went out upon deck staggering to and fro, without any further molestance from the boy. Then I look't about the beams for a marlin-speek, and seeing one hanging with a strap to a nail on the larboard side, I jerk't my right arm forth and back, which clear'd the two men's hands from my right arm, and took hold of the marlin-speek, and struck the point four times, about a quarter of an inch deep into the skull of that man that had hold of my left arm, before they took hold of my right arm again. And I struck the marlin-speek three times into his head after they had hold of me, which caused him to screech out, but they having hold of me, took off much of the force of the three blows, and being a strong-hearted man, he would not let go his hold of me, and the two men, finding that my right arm was stronger than their four arms were, and observing the strap of the marlin-speek to fall up and down upon the back of my hand, one of them let go his right hand and took hold of the strap and haul'd the marlin-speek out of my hand, and I, fearing what in all likelihood would follow, I put my right hand before my head as a guard, although three hands had hold of that arm; for I concluded he would knock me on the head with it; but, through God's providence it fell out of his hand and so close to the ship's side that he could not reach it again without letting go his other hand from mine, so he took hold of my arm with the other hand again.

"At this time the Almighty God gave me strength enough to take one man in one hand, and throw at the other's head. Then it pleased God to put me in mind of my knife in my pocket, and although two of the men had hold of my right arm, yet God Almighty strengthened me so that I put my right hand into my pocket, and took out my knife and sheath, holding it behind my hand that they should not see it; but I could not draw it out of the sheath with my left hand, because the man that I struck on the head with the marlin-speek had still hold of it, with his back to my breast; so I put it between my legs, and drew it out, and then cut the man's throat with it, that had his back to my breast, and he immediately dropt down, and scarce ever stirr'd after.

Then with my left arm I gave both the men a push from me, and haul'd my right arm with a jerk to me, and so clear'd it of both of them; and fetching a strike with intent to cut both their throats at once, they immediately apprehended the danger they were in, put their hands together and held them up, crying, 'Corte, corte (i.e. Quarter), Mounseer, moy allay par Angleterre si vou plea.' With that I stopt my hand, and said good quarter you shall have. 'Alle a pro' ('Go to the fore') and then I put up my knife into the sheath again.

"Then I made fast the steerage door, and ordered the boy to stand by it, and keep it fast, and to look through the blunderbuss holes, and if he did see any man coming towards the door, to tell me of it, and come into the cabin for the blunderbuss and ammunition which I had hid away before we were taken.

"After that I had loaden, I came out with it into the steerage and look't forward, out of the companion, to see if any man did lie over the steerage door – but seeing no man there, I went out upon deck and look't up to the maintop, for fear the two wounded men were there and should throw down anything upon my head; but seeing no man there, I asked the boy if he could tell what was become of the two wounded men that came to themselves and went out upon the deck whilst I was engaged with the three men in the steerage. The boy told me they had scrambled over-board. But I thought it very strange that they should be accessory to their own deaths. Then I ordered the boy to stand by the steerage door to see if that man betwixt decks did come up, and if he did, to tell me.

"Then I went forward to the two men that had cried for quarter, but they, being afraid, ran forward and were going up the fore-shrouds, but I held up the blunderbuss at them, and said, 'Veni abau et montea cuttelia et allez abau' ['Venez en bas, et montez le scuttle et allez en bas'] and then they put off their hats and said, 'Monsieur, moy travally pur Angleterre si vous plea'; but I answered 'Alle abau,' for I don't want any help; and then

27

they unlid the scuttle, and went down. Then I went forward, and as I came before the foot of the mainsail I look't up to the foretop, and seeing no man there, I look't down in the forecastle, and showed the two men a scuttle that went down into the forepeak, and said: 'Le monte cuttelia et ally abau.' They unlid the scuttle, and put off their hats and step't down.

"Then I call'd down to them and asked them if they saw any men betwixt decks as they went down, and they answered no. Then I call'd forward the boy and gave him the blunderbuss and bid him present it down the forecastle, and if he saw any men take hold of me, or if I call'd on him for help, then he should be sure to discharge the blunderbuss at us, and kill us all together, if he could not shoot them without me.

"Then I took the boy's bolt and put my head down the scuttle, and seeing no man there I leap't down in the forecastle and laid the scuttle and nail'd it fast, and thought myself fast, seeing two killed and two secured.

"Then I went upon deck, and took the blunderbuss from the boy and gave him the bolt, and went aft, and ordered the boy as before to stand by the steerage door, and give me an account if he saw any man come towards him with a handspike; and then I went aft into the cabin, and cut two candles in four pieces and lighted them, one I left burning upon the table, the other three I carried in my left hand, and the blunderbuss in my right hand; and I put my head down the gun-room scuttle and look't around, and seeing no man there, I leap't down and went to the man that lay all the time asleep in a cabin betwixt decks, and took him by the shoulder with my left hand, and wakened him, and presented the blunderbuss at him with my right hand, and commanded him out of his cabin, and made him stand still, till I got up into the steerage. Then I call'd the man, and he standing on the scuttle and seeing the man that had his throat cut almost buried in his blood, he wrung his hands, crying out, 'O Jesu Maria!' I told him I had nothing to do with Maria now.

'Monte, monte et allez a pro!' Then he came up and went forward looking round to see his companions, but I followed him, and made him go down into the forecastle. Then I gave the boy the blunderbuss and ordered him to present it at the man if he perceived him to come towards me while I was opening the scuttle, then to shoot him.

"Then I took the crow and leap't down with it into the forecastle and drew the spikes and opened the scuttle, and bid the man come down and join his companions. And after that I nailed down the scuttle again, and went aft and ordered the boy to stand by the steerage door again, and I took the candles and the blunderbuss and went down between decks and looked in all holes and corners for the two wounded men and found them not. Then I went on deck, and told the boy I could not find the men, and he said they were certainly run overboard. I told him I would know what was become of them before I made sail.

"Then I told the boy I would go up into the main-top, and see if they were there; and so I gave him the blunderbuss and bid him present it at the maintop, and if he saw any man look out over the top with anything in his hand to throw at me, he should then shoot them. Then I took the boy's bolt, and went up, and when I was got to the puddick shrouds I look'd forwards to the foretop. I saw the two men were cover'd with the foretopsail, and their sashes bound about their heads to keep in the blood, and they had made a great part of the foretopsail bloody, and as the ship rolled, the blood ran over the top. Then I call'd to them, and they turn'd out and went down on their knees, and wrung their hands, and cried, 'O corte, corte, Monsieur.' Then I said, 'Good quarter shall you have,' and I went down and call'd to them to come down, and he that the boy wounded came down, and kissed my hand over and over, and went down into the forecastle, very willingly. But the other man was one of the three that I designed to kill; he delayed his coming. I took the blunderbuss and said I would shoot him down, and then he came a little way and stood still, and begged me to give him quarter. I told him if he would come down he should have quarter. Then he came down and I gave the boy the blunderbuss" – and then ensued the redrawing of the nails and the reopening of the scuttle, so as to thrust these two wounded men in with the others. But Lyde called up one of the men, a fellow of about four-and-twenty, and who had shown Lyde some kindness when he was a prisoner on the ship. We need not follow Lyde in his voyage home. He made the Frenchman help to navigate the vessel. But they had still many difficulties to overcome, the weather was rough, the ship leaked, and there were but Lyde and the Frenchman and the boy to handle her.

Even when he did reach the mouth of the Exe, though he signalled for a pilot, none would come out to him, as he had no English colours on board to hoist, and he was obliged to beat about all night and next day in Torbay till the tide would serve for crossing the bar at Exmouth. Again he signalled for a pilot. The boat came out, but would approach only near enough to be hailed. Only then, when the pilot was satisfied that this was not a privateer of the enemy, would he come on board, and steer her to Starcross. Thence he sent his prisoners to Topsham in the Customs House wherry. There they were examined by the doctor, who pronounced the condition of two of them hopeless.

Lyde's troubles were by no means over; for the owners of the *Friend's Adventure* were vastly angry at her having been brought safely back. She had been insured by them for £560, and when valued was knocked down for £170; and they did much to annoy and harass Lyde, and prevent him getting another ship.

However, his story got about, and the Marquess of Carmarthen introduced him to Queen Mary, who presented him with a gold medal and chain, and recommended him to the Lords of the Admiralty for preferment in the fleet.

With this his narrative ends. He expresses his hope to serve their Majesties, and to have another whack at the Frenchmen.

Manly Peeke

The pirates of Algiers had for some years been very trouble-some, not in the Mediterranean only, but also along the European coasts of the Atlantic. Several English vessels trading to Smyrna had been plundered, and the corsairs had even made descents on the coasts of England and Ireland and had swept away people into slavery. James I proposed that the different Christian powers should unite to destroy Algiers, the principal port of these pirates. Spain, whose subjects suffered most, engaged to co-operate, but withdrew at the last moment. Sir Robert Mansell was placed in command of the English fleet, but provided with an inefficient force, and given strict orders from the timid and parsimonious James not on any account to endanger his vessels.

On 24 May, 1621, Sir Robert sailed into the harbour of Algiers and set fire to the Moorish ships and galleys; but had scarcely retired – unwilling to follow up the advantage – when "a great cataract of rain" hindered the spread of the fire; and the Algerines succeeded in recovering all their ships with the exception of two, which burnt to the water's edge. The enemy brought their artillery to bear on the English fleet, mounted batteries on the mole, and threw booms across the mouth of the harbour. Mansell, hampered by his instructions, dared not expose his vessels further and withdrew, having lost only eight men; and returned to England. Among those who had sailed with him was Richard Peeke, of Tavistock, who returned home much disgusted, "My Body more wasted and weatherbeaten, but my purse never the fuller nor my pockets thicker lined."

Charles I came to the throne in 1625; and one of his first acts was to organize and start an expedition against the Spanish. It was devised for the sake of plunder. His treasury was empty; he was obliged to borrow £3000 to procure provisions for his own table. Plate ships, heavy-laden argosies, were arriving in the port of Spain from the New World, and Buckingham suggested to him to fill his empty coffers by the capture of these vessels. The English fleet counted eighty sail; the Dutch contributed a squadron of sixteen sail; it was the greatest joint naval power that had ever spread sail upon salt water – and this made the world abroad wonder what the purpose was for which it was assembled. Ten thousand men were embarked on the English vessels, and the command of both fleet and army was given to Sir Edward Cecil, now created Lord Wimbledon, a general who had served with very little success in the Palatinate and the Low Countries. This appointment of a mere landsman surprised and vexed the seamen. The position belonged to Sir Robert Mansell, Vice-Admiral of England, in case the Admiral did not go; but Buckingham had made the choice and persisted in it. The fleet set sail in the month of October, and shaped its course for the coast of Spain.

Richard Peeke had remained in Tavistock after his return from Algiers till October, 1625, when "The drum beating up for a new expedition in which many noble gentlemen, and heroical spirits, were to venture their honours, lives and fortunes, cables could not hold me, for away I would, and along I vowed to go, and did so." Peeke entered as sailor on board the *Convertine*, under Captain Thomas Porter.

In the Bay of Biscay the ships were damaged and in part scattered by a storm. One vessel foundered with a hundred and seventy men on board. This was the beginning of misadventure. The confusion of orders was such that the officers and soldiers scarcely knew who were in command and whom they were to order about. When Wimbledon got in sight of the Spanish shores, he summoned a council of war, the usual and dangerous resource of an incompetent commander. His instructions were to intercept the plate ships from America, to scour the Spanish shores and destroy the shipping in the ports. But where should he begin? In the council of war some recommended one point, some another; in the end it was resolved to make for Cadiz Bay. But whilst they were consulting, the Spaniards had got wind of their approach, and prepared to receive them. Moreover, Wimbledon allowed seven large and rich Spanish vessels to sail into the bay under his nose, and these afterwards did him much damage. "'Tis thought," says Howell, who had many friends with the expedition, "that they being rich would have defrayed well near the charge of our fleet."

A sudden attack on the shipping at Cadiz and Port St Maria could hardly have failed even now, but the blundering and incompetent Wimbledon preferred to land all his troops, and he succeeded in capturing the paltry fort of Puntal, whilst his fleet remained inactive outside the bay. Then he moved towards the bridge which connects the Isle de Laon with the continent, to cut off communications. No enemy was visible; but in the wine-cellars of the country, which were broken open and plundered, a foe was found which has ever been more dangerous to undisciplined English troops than bullets and sabres. The men, under no control, got drunk and became totally unmanageable; and if the Spaniards had been on the alert they might have cut them to pieces. Lord Wimbledon then ordered a retreat, but this was conducted in such a manner that hundreds of stragglers were left behind to fall under the knives of the enraged peasantry.

Richard Peeke, not being a soldier, did not accompany the army; but at midday thought that he might as well also go ashore to refresh himself. He did so, and met some of the men laden with oranges and lemons. He inquired of them where the enemy was. They replied that they had not seen a Spaniard. Thereupon "we parted, they to the ships, I forward, and before I reached a mile, I found three Englishmen stark dead, being slain, lying in the way, and one, some small distance off, not fully dead." Whilst Peeke was assisting the wounded man, a Spanish cavaliero, whose name he afterwards learned was Don Juan de

33

Cadiz, came up and attacked him, but Peeke flapped his cloak in the eyes of the horse, which swerved, and Peeke mastered the Don, and threw him down. The Spaniard pleaded for mercy, and Peeke, after emptying the Don's pocket of a few coins, bade him depart. At that moment, however, up came fourteen Spanish musketeers. "Thus far, my voyage for oranges sped well, but in the end proved sour sauce to me." The musketeers overpowered Peeke, and the ungrateful Don stabbed at him, "and wounded me through the face from ear to ear, and had there killed me, had not the fourteen musketeers rescued me from his rage. Upon this I was led in triumph into the town of Cales [Cadiz]; an owl not more wondered and hooted at, a dog not more cursed. In my being led thus along the streets, a Fleming spying me cried out aloud, 'Whither do you lead this English dog? Kill him, kill him, he's no Christian.' And with that, breaking through the crowd, in upon those who held me, ran me into the body with a halbert, at the reins of my back, at least four inches."

He was taken before the Governor, who had him well treated and attended by surgeons, and when he was better, dispatched him to Xeres, which he calls Sherrys. Meanwhile his captain, Porter, induced Lord Wimbledon to send a messenger on shore and offer to ransom Peeke at any reasonable price; but the Spanish Governor, supposing him to be a man of far greater consequence than he was, refused this, and at Xeres he was had up on 15 November before a council of war, consisting of three dukes, four counts, four marquesses, and other great persons. Two Irish friars attended as interpreters. These men had been in England the year before acting as spies and bringing to Spain reports of the number of guns and troops in Plymouth. "At my first appearing before the Lords, my sword lying before them on a table, the Duke of Medina asked me if I knew that weapon. It was reached to me, I took it, and embraced it in mine arms, and with tears in mine eyes kissed the pommel of it. He then demanded, how many men I had killed with that weapon. I told him if I had killed one I had not been there now, before that princely assembly, for when I had him at my foot begging for mercy, I gave him life, yet he then very poorly did me a mischief. Then they asked Don John what wounds I gave him. He said, 'None.' Upon this he was rebuked and told that if upon our first encounter he had run me through, it had been a fair and noble triumph, but so to wound me being in the hands of others, they held it base."

He was now closely questioned as to the fleet, the number of guns in the vessels, the fortifications of Plymouth, the garrison and the ordnance there, and was greatly surprised to find how accurately the Council was informed on every point.

"By the common people who encompassed me round, many jeerings, mockeries, scorns and bitter jests were to my face thrown upon our Nation. At length one of the Spaniards called Englishmen *gallinas* (hens); at which the great lords fell a laughing. Hereupon one of the Dukes, pointing to the Spanish soldiers, bid me note how their King kept them. And indeed, they were all wondrous brave in apparel, hats, bands, cuffs, garters, etc, and some of them in chains of gold. And asked further if I thought these would prove such hens as our English, when next year they should come into England? I said no. But being somewhat emboldened by his merry countenance, I told him as merrily, I thought they would be within one degree of hens, and would prove pullets or chickens. 'Darst thou then (quoth Duke Medina, with a brow half angry) fight with one of these Spanish pullets?'

"'O my Lord,' said I, 'I am a prisoner, and my life is at stake, and therefore dare not be so bold to adventure upon any such action; yet with the license of this princely assembly, I dare hazard the breaking of a rapier; and withal told him, he was unworthy the name of an Englishman that should refuse to fight with one man of any nation whatsoever.' Hereupon my shackles were knocked off, and my iron ring and chain taken from my neck.

"Room was made for the combatants, rapier and dagger the weapons. A Spanish champion presents himself, named Señor Tiago, whom after we had played some reasonable good time, I disarmed, as thus – I caught his rapier betwixt the bar of my poignard and there held it, till I closed in with him, and tripping up his heels, I took his weapons out of his hands, and delivered them to the Dukes.

"I was then demanded, if I durst fight against another. I told them, my heart was good to adventure, but humbly requested them to give me pardon if I refused, for I too well knew that the Spaniard is haughty, impatient of the least affront, and when he receives but a touch of any dishonour, his revenge is implacable, mortal and bloody.

"Yet being by the noblemen pressed again and again to try my fortune with another, I said, that if their Graces and Greatnesses would give me leave to play at mine own country weapon, called the quarter-staff, I was then ready there, an opposite against any comer, whom they would call forth; and would willingly lay down my life before those princes, to do them service, provided my life might by no foul means be taken from me.

"Hereupon, the head of a halbert which went with a screw was taken off, and the steall [staff] delivered to me; the other butt-end of the staff having a short iron pike in it. This was my armour, and in my place I stood, expecting an opponent.

"At last, a handsome and well-spirited Spaniard steps forth with his rapier and poignard. They asked me what I said to him. I told them I had a sure friend in my hand that never failed me, and made little account of that one to play with. Then a second, armed as before, presents himself. I demanded if there would come no more. The Duke asked, how many I desired. I told them any number under six.

Which resolution of mine they smiling at it in a kind of scorn, held it not manly nor fit for their own honours and glory of their nation, to worry one man with a multitude; and therefore appointed three only to enter the lists.

"The rapier men traversed their ground, I mine. Dangerous thrusts were put in, and with dangerous hazard avoided. Shouts echoed to heaven, to encourage the Spaniards, not a shout nor a hand to hearten the poor Englishman; only Heaven I had in mine eye, the honour of my country in my heart, my fame at the stake, my life on a narrow bridge, and death both before me and behind me.

"Plucking up a good heart, seeing myself faint and wearied, I vowed to my soul to do something ere she departed from me; and so setting all upon one cast, it was my good fortune with the butt-end where the iron pike was to kill one of the three and within a few bouts after, to disarm the other two, causing one of them to fly into the army of soldiers then present, and the other for refuge fled behind the bench.

"Now was I in greater danger; for a general murmur filled the air, with threatenings at me; the soldiers especially bit their thumbs, and how was it possible for me to scape?

"Which the noble Duke of Medina Sidonia seeing called me to him, and instantly caused proclamation that none, on pain of death, should meddle with me. And by his honourable protection I got off. And not off, only, with safety, but with money, for by the Dukes and Condes were given me in gold to the value of four pounds ten shillings sterling, and by the Marquess Alquenezes himself as much; he embracing me in his arms and bestowing upon me that long Spanish russet cloak I now wear, which he took from one of his men's backs; and withal furnished me with a clean band and cuffs."

The Spaniards, nobly appreciating the bravery of their captive, and discovering that instead of being a man of great consequence he was a mere sailor before the mast, and not likely to be redeemed at a great price, resolved to give him liberty, and under the conduct of four gentlemen attached to the suite of the

Marquess Alquenezes, he was sent to Madrid to be presented to the King. During Peeke's stay in Madrid, which he calls Madrill, he was the guest of the Marquess. The Marchioness showed him great kindness, and on his leaving presented him with a gold chain and jewels for his wife, and pretty things for his children. On Christmas Day he was presented to the King, the Queen, and Don Carlos, the Infante.

"Being brought before him, I fell (as it was fit) on my knees. Many questions were demanded of me, which so well as my plain wit directed me, I resolved.

"In the end, his Majesty offered me a yearly pension (to a good value) if I would serve him, either at land or at sea; for which his royal favour, I confessing myself infinitely bound, most humbly entreated, that with his princely leave, I might be suffered to return into mine own country, being a subject only to the King of England my sovereign.

"And besides that bond of allegiance there was another obligation due from me, to a wife and children. And therefore most submissively begged, that his Majesty would be so princely minded as to pity my estate and to let me go. To which he at last granted, bestowing upon me, one hundred pistoletts, to bear my charges.

"Having thus left Spain, I took my way through some part of France, and hoisting sail for England I landed on the 23rd day of April, 1626, at Foy in Cornwall."

Whilst Peeke was in Spain, Lord Wimbledon had been blundering with his fleet and army worse than before. After he had reshipped his army, there still remained the hope of intercepting the plate fleet, but an infectious disorder broke out in the ships of Lord Delaware, and in consequence of an insane order given by Wimbledon, that the sick should be distributed into the healthy ships, the malady spread. After beating about for eighteen days with a dreadful mortality on board, and without catching a glimpse of the treasure vessels from the New World,

Lord Wimbledon resolved to carry his dishonoured flag home again, "which was done in a confused manner, and without any observance of sea orders." The plate fleet, which had been hugging the coast of Barbary, appeared off the coast of Spain two or three days after his departure, and entered safely into the harbour of Cadiz. Moreover, whilst he was master of these seas, a fleet of fifty sail, laden with treasure, got safe into Lisbon, from Brazil. With the troops and crews dreadfully reduced in numbers, with sickness and discontent in every vessel, and without a single prize of the least value, Lord Wimbledon arrived in Plymouth Sound, to be hissed and hooted by the indignant people, and to have his name of Cecil ridiculed as Sit-still. This sorry and unsuccessful expedition which had cost Charles so much was a grievous blow to him. A thousand men had perished in the expedition, a great sum of money had been thrown away, and the whole country was roused to anger. The Privy Council was convened and an examination into the miscarriage was instituted, but the statements of the officers were discordant, their complaints reciprocal, and after a long investigation, it was deemed expedient to bury the whole matter in silence.

It has been well said, that the only man who of the whole expedition came out with credit to himself and to his country was Richard Peeke, of Tavistock, who earned for himself the epithet of "Manly".

What became of Peeke afterwards we do not know; in the troubles of the Civil War he doubtless played a part, and almost certainly on the side of the Crown. The authority for the story is a rare pamphlet by Peeke himself, entitled, *Three to One, Being, An English-Spanish Combat, Performed by a Westerne Gentleman, of Tavystoke in Devonshire, with an English Quarter-Staffe, against Three Spanish Rapiers and Poniards, at Sherries in Spain, The fifteene day of November, 1625...* the Author of this Booke, and Actor in this Encounter, Richard Peeke.

Joseph Pitts

Joseph Pitts, of Exeter, was the son of John Pitts of that city. When aged fourteen or fifteen he became a sailor. After two or three voyages, very short, he shipped on board the *Speedwell,* on Easter Tuesday, 1678, at Lympston, bound for the Western Islands, from thence to Newfoundland, thence to Bilbao, and so by the Canaries, home. Newfoundland was reached, but on the voyage to Bilbao the ship was boarded and taken by Algerine pirates.

"The very first words they spake, and the very first thing they did was beating us with ropes, saying: 'Into boat, you English dogs!' and without the least opposition, with fear, we tumbled into their boat, we scarce knew how. They having loaded their boat, carried us aboard their ship, and diligent search was made about us for money, but they found none. We were the first prize they had taken for that voyage, and they had been out at sea about six weeks. As for our vessel, after they had taken out of her what they thought fit and necessary for their use, they sunk her; for she being laden with fish, they thought it not worth while to carry her home to Algier.

"About four or five days after our being thus taken, they met with another small English ship, with five or six men aboard, which was served as ours was. And two or three days after that, they espied another small English vessel, with five or six men aboard laden with fish, and coming from New England. This vessel was at their first view of her some leagues at windward of them, and there being but little wind, and so they being out of hopes of getting up to her, they us'd this cunning device, they hauled up their sails, and hang'd out our English King's colours, and so appearing man-of-war-like decoyed her down, and sunk her also.

"Two or three days after this, they took a fourth little English ship with four or five men a-board laden with herrings, of which they took out most part, and then sunk the ship."

The pirates now returned to Algiers, and their captured Christians were driven to the palace of the Dey, who had a right to select an eighth of them for the public service and also to retain an eighth part of the spoils taken from the prizes. His selection being made, the rest were driven to the market-place and put up to auction.

Joseph Pitts was bought by one Mustapha, who treated him with excessive barbarity.

"Within eight and forty hours after I was sold, I tasted of their (Algerine) cruelty; for I had my tender feet tied up, and beaten twenty or thirty blows, for a beginning. And thus was I beaten for a considerable time, every two or three days, besides blows now and then, forty, fifty, sixty, at a time. My executioner would fill his pipe, and then give me ten or twenty blows, and then stop and smoke his pipe for a while, and then he would at me again, and when weary stop again; and thus cruelly would he handle me till his pipe was out. At other times he would hang me up by neck and heels, and then beat me miserably. Sometimes he would hang me up by the armpits, beating me all over my body. And oftentimes hot brine was order'd for me to put my feet into, after they were sore with beating, which put me to intolerable smart. Sometimes I have been beaten on my feet so long, and cruelly, that the blood hath run down my feet to the ground. I have oftentimes been beaten by my Patroon so violently on my breech, that it hath been black all over, and very much swollen, and hard almost as a board; insomuch, that I have not been able to sit for a considerable time."

After two or three months, Mustapha sent him to sea in a pirate vessel, in which he was interested, to attend on the gunner. The expedition was not very successful, as only one ship was taken, a Portuguese, with a crew of eighteen who were enslaved. On his return to Algiers, after having been a couple of months at sea, he was sold to a second "Patroon", named Ibrahim, who had "two brothers in Algiers and a third in Tunis. The middle brother had designed to make a voyage to Tunis to see his brother there; and it seems I was bought in order to be given as a present to him. I was then cloth'd very fine, that I might be the better accepted. The ship being ready we put to sea, and in about fourteen days time we arrived at Tunis, and went forthwith to my Patroon's brother's house. The next day my Patroon's brother's son, taking a pride to have a Christian to wait upon him, made me walk after him. As I was attending upon my new Master through the streets, I met with a gentleman habited like a Christian, not knowing him to be an Englishman, as he was. He look'd earnestly upon me, and ask'd me whether I were not an Englishman. I answered him, Yea! How came you hither? said he. I told him I came with my Patroon. What, are you a slave? said he. I replied, yes. But he was loath to enter into any further discourse with me in the public street, and therefore desired of the young man on whom I waited, that he would please to bring me to his house. The young man assured him he would; for being a drinker of wine, and knowing the plenty of it in the said gentleman's house, he was the rather willing to go. After the gentleman was gone from us, my young new master told me, that he whom we talk'd to was the English Consul."

The Consul kindly invited Joseph Pitts to go to his house as often as he had an opportunity. After spending thirty days in Tunis, Pitts learned to his dismay that the "Patroon's brother" did not care to have him, and that consequently he would have to return to Algiers. The Consul and two merchants then endeavoured to buy Pitts, but his master demanded for him five hundred dollars; they offered three hundred, which was all that they could afford, and as Ibrahim refused to sell at this price, the negotiation was broken off, and he returned with his master to Algiers.

Here he was subjected to the persecution of his master's

youngest brother, who endeavoured to induce Joseph to become a renegade. As persuasion availed nothing, the young man went to his elder brother Ibrahim, and told him that he had been a profligate and debauched man in his time, as also a murderer; and that his only chance of paradise lay in making atonement for his iniquities by obtaining or enforcing the conversion of his slave.

Ibrahim was alarmed, and being a superstitious man believed this, and began to use great cruelty towards Pitts. "He call'd two of his servants, and commanded them to tie up my feet with a rope to the post of the tent; and when they had so done, he with a great cudgel fell to beating of me upon my bare feet. He being a very strong man, and full of passion, his blows fell heavy indeed; and the more he beat the more chafed and enraged he was; and declared, that if I would not turn, he would beat me to death. I roar'd out to feel the pains of his cruel strokes; but the more I cry'd, the more furiously he laid on upon me; and to stop the noise of my crying, he would stamp with his feet on my mouth; at which I beg'd him to despatch me out of the way; but he continued beating me. After I had endured this merciless usage so long, till I was ready to faint and die under it, and saw him as mad and implacable as ever, I beg'd him to forbear and I would turn. And breathing a while, but still hanging by the feet, he urg'd me again to speak the words, yet loath I was, and held him in suspense awhile; and at length told him that I could not speak the words. At which he was more enrag'd than before, and fell at me again in a most barbarous manner. After I had received a great many blows a second time, I beseech'd him again to hold his hand, and gave him fresh hopes of my turning Mohammetan; and after I had taken a little more breath, I told him as before, I could not do what he desired. And thus I held him in suspense three or four times; but, at last, seeing his cruelty towards me insatiable, unless I did turn Mohammetan, through terror I did it, and spake the words, holding up the

43

fore-finger of my right-hand; and presently I was led away to a fire, and care was taken to heal my feet (for they were so beaten, that I was unable to go on them for several days), and so I was put to bed."

Algiers was bombarded thrice by the French whilst Joseph Pitts was living there as a slave, their purpose being to obtain the surrender of French captives who had been enslaved.

"They then threw but few bombs into the town, and that by night; nevertheless the inhabitants were so surprized and terrified at it, being unacquainted with bombs, that they threw open the gates of the city, and men, women, and children left the town. Whereupon the French had their country-men, that were slaves, for nothing. In a little while after the French came again to Algiers, upon other demands, and then the Dey surrendered up all the French slaves, which prov'd the said Dey's ruin. And then they came a third time (1682). There were nine bomb-vessels, each having two mortars, which kept firing day and night insomuch that there would be five or six bombs flying in the air at once. At this the Algerines were horribly enrag'd, and to be reveng'd, fired away from the mouth of their cannon about forty French slaves, and finding that would not do, but d'Estrée (the Marshall) was rather the more enraged. They sent for the French Consul, intending to serve him the same sauce. He pleaded his character, and that 'twas against the Law of Nations, etc. They answered, they were resolv'd, and all these compliments would not serve his turn. At which he desir'd a day or two's respite, till he should despatch a letter to the Admiral. Which was granted him; and a boat was sent out with a white flag. But after the Admiral had perused and considered the Consul's letter, he bid the messenger return this answer: That his commission was to throw 10,000 bombs into the town, and he would do it to the very last, and that as for the Consul, if he died, he could not die better than for his prince.

"This was bad news to the Consul; and highly provoked the

Algerines, who immediately caused the Consul to be brought down and placed him before the mouth of a cannon, and fired him off also."

D'Estrée's success was by no means so great as he had anticipated and as was expected. He was compelled by the stubborn defence of Algiers to content himself with an exchange of prisoners for French slaves, nor did he recover more than forty or fifty.

Meanwhile, what was the English Government doing for the protection of its subjects, for the recovery of Englishmen who were languishing as slaves in Algiers and Tunis? Nothing at all.

Under the Commonwealth, Blake in 1654 had severely chastised the nest of pirates. He had compelled the Dey to restrain his piratical subjects from further violence against the English. He had presented himself before Tunis, where, incensed by the violence of the Dey, he had destroyed the castles of Porto Farino and Goletta, had sent a numerous detachment of sailors in their long-boats into the harbour, and burned every vessel which lay there.

But now the despicable Charles II was king, and the power of England to protect its subjects was sunk to impotence. Every three years the English fleet appeared off Algiers to renew a treaty of peace with the Dey, that meant nothing; the piratical expeditions continued, and Englishmen were allowed to remain groaning in slavery, tortured into acceptance of Mohammedanism, and not a finger was raised for their protection and release. The Consuls were impotent. They could do nothing. There was no firm government behind them.

In Algiers, Pitts met with an Englishman, James Grey, of Weymouth, with whom he became intimate. This man often appealed to Pitts for advice, whether he should turn Mussulman or not; but Pitts would give him no counsel one way or the other. Finally, he became a renegade, but moped, lost all heart, and died.

Pitts tells us how that secretly he received a letter from his father, advising him "to have a care and keep close to God, and to be sure, never, by any methods of cruelty that could be used towards him, to deny his blessed Saviour; and that he – his father – would rather hear of his son's death than of his becoming a Mahommedan." The letter was slipped into his hands a few days after he had become a renegade. He dared to show this to his master, and told him frankly, "I am no Turk, but a Christian." The master answered, "If you say this again, I will have a fire made, and burn you in it immediately."

The then Dey, Baba Hasan, died in 1683, and Pitts' master being rich and having friends, attempted a revolt against Hasein "Mezzomorto", his successor, and was killed in the attempt. This led to the sale of Pitts again, and he was bought by an old bachelor, named Eumer, a kindly old man, with whom he was happy. "My work with him was to look after his house, to dress his meat, to wash his clothes; and, in short, to do all those things that are look'd on as servant-maids' work in England." With the old master he made the pilgrimage to Mecca, and thence went on to Medina, and he was the first Englishman to give a description of these sacred towns. Moreover, his account is remarkably exact. He was a young fellow full of observation and intelligence, and he made good use of his eyes. At Mecca, Eumer gave Pitts his freedom, and Pitts remained with him, not any longer as a slave, but as a servant.

By being granted his freedom this did not involve the liberty to return to his home and his Christian religion. But he looked out anxiously for an opportunity to do both. This came in a message arriving from Constantinople from the Sultan to demand the assistance of Algerine vessels, and Joseph Pitts volunteered as a seaman upon one of these vessels, in the vain hope of its being captured by some Christian vessel – French, for there was nothing to be expected from English ships.

At Algiers, he became acquainted with a Mr Butler, and as

Pitts was suffering from sore eyes, Mr Butler got an English doctor, who was a slave, to attend to him and cure him. Mr Butler introduced him to the English Consul, whom he saw once, and once only, and who could do nothing for him further than give him a letter to the English Consul at Smyrna, at the same time imploring him to conceal the letter and not let it get into the hands of the Turks, or it might cost him his life.

"Being got about thirty days' voyage towards Smyrna, where I design'd to make my escape, we espied seven or eight Venetian galleys at anchor under the shore. The Turks had a great tooth for these galleys, but knew not how to come to them, not being able to adventure so far as galleys safely may. At length they consulted, being fifteen ships in number, to hoist French colours. Having done this we haul'd up our sails and brought to, pretending as if we were desirous of some news from the Levant. They, at this, thinking we were French men-of-war, sent out two of their galleys; upon which the Turks were ordered to lie close, and not stir, for fear of showing their turbants, and such officers, that were obliged to be moving, took off their turbants to avoid discovery, and put on a hat and cap instead thereof; but the slaves were all ordered to be upon deck to colour the matter, and make us look more like Christians. At length one of the galleys being within musket-shot, we fired upon him, and soon made him strike. The other, seeing that, turns and rows with all his might and main to get ashore, the Algerines all the while making what sail they could after him, but 'twas in vain, for the Venetian got clear, the wind being off shore just in our mouth. In that galley which we took, there were near four hundred Christians, and some few Turks that were slaves.

"When we came to Scio, we were join'd with ten sail of the Grand Turk's ships, carrying seventy or eighty brass cannon guns each; and now being twenty-five in number, we had the courage to cruise about the Islands of the archipelago.

Some time after we arrived at Scio, the Turks had liberty, for one month's time, to go home to visit the respective places of their nativity. I went to Smyrna and hired a chamber there. And after I knew where the Consul's house was I went thither. The Consul not knowing who I was, complimented me much, because I was handsomely apparel'd, and I returned the compliment to him after the Turkish manner; and then delivered him my letter of recommendation. The Consul, having perused the letter, he bid the interpreter to withdraw, because he should not understand anything of the matter. After the interpreter was gone, the Consul ask'd me whether I was the man mentioned in the letter. I told him I was. He said the design was very dangerous, and that if it should be known to the Turks that he was any way concerned in it, it was as much as his life, and his all was worth. But after he had discoursed with me further and found I was fully resolv'd in the matter, he told me that truly were it not for Mr Butler's request he would not meddle in such a dangerous attempt; but for the friendship and respect he bore to him, would do me all the kindness he could; which put life into me.

"We had no English nor Dutch ships at Smyrna then, but daily expected some; and he told me, I must wait till they came, and withall caution'd me not to frequent his house. A day or two after this I was sitting in a barber's shop, where both Christians and Turks did trim, and there was a-trimming then an English man, whose name was George Grunsell, of Deptford. He knew me no otherwise than a Turk; but when I heard him speak English, I ask'd him in English, whether he knew any from the Western parts of England to be in Smyrna. He told me of one, who he thought was an Exeter man, which, when I heard, I was glad at heart. I desired him to show me his house; which he very kindly did; but when I came to speak with Mr Elliott, for so was his name, I found him to be of Cornwall, who had serv'd some part of his apprenticeship in Exon, with Mr Henry Cudmore a merchant. He was very glad to see me for country's-sake. After some discourse, I communicated to him my design. He was very glad to hear of it, and promised to assist me; and told me, that I need not run the hazard of going to the Consul's house, but that if I had anything of moment to impart to him, he would do it for me.

"In a month's time it was cry'd about the city of Smyrna, that all Algerines should repair to their ships, which lay then at Rhodes.

"All this while no English or Dutch ships came to Smyrna; the Consul and Mr Elliott therefore consulted which was my best way to take; to tarry in Smyrna after all the Algerines were gone, would look suspiciously; and therefore they advised me not to tarry in Smyrna, but either to go to Scio with the Algerines, which is part of our way back to Rhodes, or else to go up to Constantinople; and when I was there, to write to the said Mr Elliott to acquaint him where I was; and to stay there till I had directions from them to return to Smyrna, or what else to do.

"I pursued their advice, and went with some of the Algerines to Scio, and there I made a stop till all the Algerines were gone from thence, and writ to Mr Elliott where I was. A short time after, he writ me, that he was very glad that I was where I was, but withal, gave a damp to my spirits, with this bad news, that our Smyrna fleet were said to be interrupted by the French; with the cold reserve of comfort, that it wanted confirmation.

"Now the Devil was very busy with me, tempting me to lay aside all thoughts of escaping, and to return to Algiers, and continue Mussulman. For it was suggested to me, first, that it was a very difficult, if not a desperate attempt, to endeavour to make my escape; and that if I were discovered in it, I should be put to death after the most cruel and exemplary way. Also, in the next place, the loss that I should sustain thereby, in several respects, viz. the loss of the profitable returns which I might make of what money I had to Algiers; and the loss of receiving eight months pay due to me in Algiers; and the frustrating of my hopes and expectation which I had from my Patroon, who made me large promises of leaving me considerable substance at his death; and I believe he meant as he promised; for I must acknowledge he was like a father to me.

"In the midst of all I would pray to God for his assistance, and found it. For I bless God, that after all my acquaintance were gone from Scio to Rhodes, I grew daily better and better satisfied; though my fears were still very great; and I was indeed afraid everybody I met did suspect my design. And I can truly say, that I would not go through such a labyrinth of sorrows and troubles again, might I gain a kingdom.

"The first letter that Mr Elliott sent me while I was at Scio, he directed to a Greek at Scio, who did business with the Consul at Smyrna, to be delivered to me, naming me by my Turkish name. I was altogether unknown to the Greek, so that he was forced to enquire among the Algerines for one of that name; and indeed there were two men of that name with myself; but by good hap, they were gone to Rhodes, otherwise 'tis odds but the letter had come to the hands of one of them, and then my design had been discovered, and I should undoubtedly have been put to death.

"I receiv'd another letter from Mr Elliott, in which he informed me that the reported bad news concerning our ships was true, but that he and the Consul had conferr'd that day what was best to be done for my safety; and were of opinion that it would be in vain for me to wait for any English ships, and therefore they advised me to go off in a French ship, tho' somewhat more expensive, and in order thereto, to hasten back again to Smyrna, in the first boat that came.

"Accordingly I came to Smyrna again and lodg'd at Mr Grunsell's house, and kept myself very private for the space of twenty days, 'till the French ship was ready to sail.

"Now the French ship, in which I was to make my escape, was intended to sail the next day, and therefore in the evening I went on board, apparel'd as an English man, with my beard shaven, a campaign periwig, and a cane in my hand, accompanied with three or four of my friends in the boat. As we were going into the boat, there were some Turks of Smyrna walking by, but they smelt nothing of the matter. My good friend Mr Elliott had agreed with the captain of the ship to pay four pounds for my passage to Leghorn, but neither the captain nor any of the French men knew who I was. My friends, next morning, brought wine and victuals aboard; upon which they were very merry, but, for my part, I was very uneasy till the ship had made sail. I pretended myself ignorant of all foreign languages, because I would not be known to the French, who – if we had met with any Algerines – I was afraid would be so far from showing me any favour so as to conceal me, would readily discover me.

"We had a month's passage from Smyrna to Leghorn, and I was never at rest in my mind till we came to Leghorn, where, as soon as ever I came ashore, I prostrated myself, and kissed the earth, blessing Almighty God for his mercy and goodness to me, that I once more set footing on the European, Christian part of the world."

Arrived at Leghorn, Joseph Pitts was put in quarantine, but for five-and-twenty days only. Whilst in the lazaret he met with some Dutchmen, one of whom had been a near neighbour in Algiers. He suggested that Pitts should join company with him and his party travelling homewards by land. To this Joseph agreed, and they all set off at Christmas, in frosty weather, and travelled for twenty days through heavy snow. After a while Joseph's leg gave way, and he could not proceed with the others. They were constrained to leave him behind, for fear that their money would run short.

After having travelled two hundred miles in their company, he was now forced to travel five hundred on foot through Germany alone. One day as he was passing through a wood he was attacked by a party of German soldiers, who robbed him of his money.

Happily, they did not strip him and so discover that he had a good deal more than was in his pockets sewn into a belt about his waist.

"When I came to Franckfort, the gates of the city were just ready to be shut, and I offering to go in, the sentinel demanded of me who I was. I told them I was an Englishman. They bid me show my passport, but I had none. I having therefore no pass, they would not let me into the city. So the gate was shut. I sat down upon the ground and wept, bewailing my hard fortune and their unkindness, having not a bit of bread to eat, nor fire to warm myself in the extreme cold season which then was.

"But there being just outside the gate a little hut, where the soldiers kept guard, the corporal seeing me in such a condition as I was, called me in, where they had a good fire, and he gave me some of his victuals; for which seasonable kindness I gave him some money to fetch us some good liquor. And I told the corporal, if he would get me into the city the next day, I would requite him for it. Accordingly he did. He brought me to a Frenchman's house, who had a son that lived in England some time, and was lately come home again, who made me very welcome. He ask'd me what my business was; I told him 'twas to get a pass to go safe down the river (for they are so strict there in time of war, that they'll even examine their own countrymen) and withal, desired him to change a pistole for me, and to give me instead of it such money as would pass current down the river. For (as I told him) I have sometimes chang'd a pistole, and before the exchange of it had been expended in my travels, some of the money would not pass current. He chang'd my pistole for me, and told me what money would pass in such a place, and what in such a place, and what I should reserve last to pass in Holland. And he was moreover so civil, as to go to the public office and obtain a pass for me. After which he brought me to his house again, and caused one of his servants to direct me to an inn, where I should quarter, and bid me come again to him the next morning, when he sent his servant to call me, and also to pay off my host, but I had paid him before, for which he show'd dislike. After all which, he conducted me to the river's side where was a boatful of passengers ready to go to Mentz. This obliging gentleman (whose name was Van der Luh'r) told the master of the boat, that he would satisfy him for my passage to Mentz; and moreover desired an acquaintance of his in the boat to take care of me; and when at Mentz, to direct me to such a merchant, to whom he gave a letter, and therewith a piece of money to drink his health.

"When we came to Mentz, we were every man to produce his passport; and as the passes were looking over, the person in the boat, who was desired to take care of me, sent a boy to call the merchant to whom I was to deliver the letter; who immediately came, and invited me to his house.

"It hap'ned that this gentleman was a slave in Algier at the same time I was. He enquired of me about his Patroon, whom I knew very well; and we talk'd about many other things relating to Algier. I received much kindness and hospitality from the gentleman; he paid off my quarters for that night; and also gave me victuals and money, and paid for my passage from Mentz to Cologne; and moreover, sent by me a letter of recommendation to his correspondent there.

"At Cologne I received the like kindness, and had my passage paid to Rotterdam; and if I would, I might have had a letter of recommendation to some gentleman there too; but I refus'd it (with hearty thanks for the offer) being loath to be too troublesome to my friends.

"I found great kindness at Rotterdam and Helversluyce, whither our English packet-boats arrive. But when I came into England, my own native country, here I was very badly treated; for the very first night that I lay in England, I was impressed for to go in the King's service. And notwithstanding that I made known my condition, and used many arguments for my liberty, with tears, yet all this would not prevail, but away I must; and was carried to Colchester Prison, where I lay some days. While I was in prison I writ a letter to Sir William Falkener, one of the Smyrna Company in London, on whom I had a bill for a little money; he immediately got a protection for me, and sent it me, which was not only my present discharge, but prevented all further trouble to me on my road homeward, which otherwise I must unavoidably have met with.

"When I came from Colchester to London, I made it my business, as in duty bound, to go and pay my thanks to the honourable gentleman, from whom I received fresh kindness. After this I made what haste I could to dear Exeter, where I safely came, to the great joy of my friends and relations.

"I was in Algier above fifteen years. After I went out of Topsham, it was about half a year before I was taken a slave. And after I came out of Algier it was well nigh twelve months ere I could reach home."

This interesting narrative is from *A true and faithful Account of the Religion and manners of the Mohammetans. In which is a particular relation of their Pilgrimage to Mecca* by Joseph Pitts of Exon. Exon, 1704. A second edition was published at Exeter in 1717 and a third edition corrected, at London, in 1731.

Richard Parker, the Mutineer

For the story of Richard Parker, I shall quote almost verbatim the account, which is very detailed, by Camden Pelham in *Chronicles of Crime*, London, 1840.

In the year 1797, when the threatening aspect of affairs abroad made the condition of the naval force a matter of vital importance to Britain, several alarming mutinies broke out among the various fleets stationed around the shores of the country. In April of the year mentioned, the seamen of the grand fleet lying at Portsmouth disowned the authority of their officers, seized upon the ships, hoisted the red flag, and declared their determination not to lift an anchor, or obey any orders whatsoever, until certain grievances of which they complained were redressed.

There is no denying or concealing the fact – the men had been ill-paid, ill-fed, shamefully neglected by the country, which depended upon them for its all, and, in many instances, harshly and brutally treated by their officers, and belly-pinched and plundered by their pursers. They behaved with exemplary moderation. The mutineers allowed all frigates with convoys to sail, in order not to injure the commerce of the country. The delegates of the vessels drew up and signed a petition to Parliament and another to the Admiralty; their language was respectful, and their demands were very far from exorbitant.

After some delay, satisfactory concessions were made to them by Government, and the men returned to their duty. But the spirit of insubordination had spread among other squadrons in the service, and about the middle of May, immediately after the Portsmouth fleet had sailed peaceably for the Bay of Biscay, the seamen of the large fleet lying at the Nore broke out also into open mutiny. The most conspicuous personage in the insurrection was one Richard Parker, a native of Exeter, privately baptized, in St Mary Major parish, 24 April, 1767. His father was a baker in that parish, and had his shop near the turnstile. It was afterwards burnt down. He rented it of the dean and chapter, from 1761 to 1793, and acquired a little land near to Exeter as his own. Young Parker received a good education, and at the age of twelve went to sea. He served in the Royal Navy as midshipman and master's mate. But he threw up his profession on his marriage with Anne McHardy, a young woman resident in Exeter, but of Scottish origin, a member of a respectable family in Aberdeen.

This connection led Parker to remove to Scotland, where he embarked in some mercantile speculations that proved unsuccessful. The issue was that before long he found himself in embarrassed circumstances, and unable to maintain his wife and two children. In Edinburgh, where these difficulties arose, he had no friends to whom he could apply for assistance, and in a moment of desperation he took the King's bounty, and became a common sailor on board a tender at Leith. When he announced to his wife the steps he had taken, she hastened to Aberdeen in great distress to procure from her brother the means of hiring two seamen as substitutes for her husband. But when she returned with the money from Aberdeen it was too late, for the tender had just sailed with her husband on board. Her grief was aggravated at this time by the loss of one of her children. Parker's sufferings were shown to be equally acute by his conduct when the vessel sailed; crying out that he saw the body of his child floating upon the waves, he leaped overboard, and was with difficulty rescued and restored to life.

In the early days of May, 1797, Parker reached the Nore, a point of land dividing the mouth of the Thames and the Medway. Probably on account of his former experience as a seaman, he was drafted on board the *Sandwich*, the guardship that bore the flag of Admiral Buckner, the Port Admiral. The mutinous spirit which afterwards broke out certainly existed on board the Nore squadron before Parker's arrival.

Communications were kept up in secret between the various crews, and the mischief was gradually drawing to a head. But though he did not originate the feeling of insubordination, the ardent temper, boldness, and superior intelligence of Parker soon became known to his comrades, and he became a prominent man among them. Their plans being at last matured, the seamen rose simultaneously against their officers, and deprived them of their arms, as well as of all command in the ships, though behaving respectfully to them in all other ways. Each vessel was put under the government of a committee of twelve men, and, to represent the whole body of seamen, every man-of-war appointed two delegates and each gunboat one to act for the common good. Of these delegates Richard Parker was chosen president, and in an unhappy hour for himself he accepted the office.

The representative body drew up a list of grievances, of which they demanded the removal, offering return immediately after to their duty. The demands were for increased pay, better and more abundant food, a more equal division of prize money, liberty to go on shore, and prompt payment of arrears. A committee of naval inquiry subsequently granted almost all their demands, thereby acknowledging their justice. Parker signed these documents, and they were published over the whole kingdom with his name attached, as well as presented to Port Admiral Buckner, through whom they were sent to the Government. When these proceedings commenced the mutineers were suffered to go on shore, and they paraded the streets of Sheerness, where lay a part of the fleet, with music and the red flag flying.

But on 22 May, troops were sent to Sheerness to put a stop to these demonstrations. Being thus confined to their ships, the mutineers, having come to no agreement with Admiral Buckner, began to take more decisive measures for extorting compliance with their demands, as well as for securing their own safety. The vessels at Sheerness moved down to the Nore, and the combined force of the insurgents, which consisted of twenty-five sail, proceeded to block up the Thames, by refusing a free passage, up or down, to the London trade. Foreign vessels, and a few small craft, were suffered to go by, after having received a passport, signed by Richard Parker, as president of the delegates.

In a day or two the mutineers had an immense number of vessels under detention. The mode in which they kept them was as follows: the ships of war were ranged in a line, at considerable distances from each other, and in the interspaces were placed the merchant vessels, having the broadsides of the men-of-war pointed to them. The appearance of the whole assemblage is described as having been at once grand and appalling. The red flag floated from the mast-head of every one of the mutineer ships.

The Government, however, though unable at the moment to quell the mutiny by force, remained firm in their demand of "unconditional surrender as a necessary preliminary to any intercourse." This was, perhaps, the best line of conduct that could have been adopted. The seamen, to their great honour, never seemed to think of assuming an offensive attitude, and were thereby left in quiet to meditate on the dangerous position in which they stood in hostility to their own country. Disunion began to manifest itself, and Parker's efforts to revive the cooling ardour of the mutineers resulted in rousing particular hostility against himself.

Meanwhile, formidable preparations had been made by the Government for the protection of the coast against a boat attack by the mutineers, and to prevent the fleet advancing up the Thames and menacing London. All the buoys and beacons in the three channels giving entrance to the Thames had been removed. Batteries with furnaces for red-hot shot were constructed at several points. Sheerness was filled with troops, and at more distant places outposts were established to prevent the landing of parties of the mutineers. Two ships of the line, some frigates, and between twenty and thirty gunboats lying higher up the river were fitted out in great haste, to co-operate, in the event of an attack by the mutinous fleet, with the squadron from Spithead, that had been summoned. Alarm and perplexity disorganized the council of the mutineers. The supply of provisions had for some time been running short.

A price had been set on Parker's head – £500. It was thought that he might attempt to escape, and therefore a description of him was published: "Richard Parker is about thirty years of age, wears his own hair, which is black, untied, though not cropt; about five feet nine or ten inches high; has a rather prominent nose, dark eyes and complexion, and thin visage; is generally slovenly dressed, in a plain blue half-worn coat and a whitish or light coloured waistcoat and half-boots."

But Parker made no attempt to escape. The mutineering vessels held together till 30 May, when the *Clyde* frigate was carried off by a combination of its officers and some of the seamen, and was followed by the *S. Fiorenzo*. These vessels were fired upon by the mutineers, but escaped up the river. The loss was, however, more than counterbalanced by the arrival of eight ships from the mutinous fleet of Admiral Duncan, anchored in Yarmouth Roads.

On 4 June, the King's birthday, the Nore fleet showed that their loyalty to their Sovereign was undisturbed by firing a general salute.

On 6 June two more ships deserted under the fire of the whole fleet, but the same evening four more arrived from Admiral Duncan's fleet. On this day Lord Northesk, having been summoned on board the *Sandwich*, found the council, comprising sixty delegates, sitting in the state cabin, with Parker at its head. After receiving a letter containing proposals of accommodation to which the unfortunate Parker still put his name as president,

Lord Northesk left, charged to deliver this letter to the King. The answer was a refusal to all concessions till the mutineers had surrendered unconditionally. Disunion thereupon became more accentuated, and on 10 June, Parker was compelled to shift his flag to the *Montague* and the council removed with him.

On the same day the merchantmen were permitted by common consent to pass up the river, and such a multitude of ships certainly had never before entered a port by one tide.

Fresh desertions now occurred every day, and all hope of concerted action was ended by stormy discussions, in which contradictory suggestions were made with such heat as to lead in many instances to acts of violence. Upon ship after ship the red flag was hauled down and replaced by one that was white, signifying submission. On the 12th only seven ships had the red flag flying. Such was the confusion, every crew being divided into two hostile parties, that five ships were taken up the Thames by those in favour of surrender, aided by their opponents under the belief that an attack was about to be made on the shore defences. The discovery by the latter that they were betrayed aroused terrible strife.

The deck of the *Iris* frigate became a battlefield; one party in the fore, the others in the after-part, turned the great guns against each other, and fought till the mutineers were worsted.

By the 16th the mutiny had terminated, every ship having been restored to the command of its officers. A party of soldiers went on board the *Sandwich* to which Parker had returned, and to them the officers surrendered the delegates of the ship, namely a man named Davies and Richard Parker.

Richard Parker, to whom the title of admiral had been accorded by the fleet and by the public during the whole of this affair, was the undoubted ringleader, and was the individual on whom all eyes were turned as the chief of the mutineers. He was brought to trial on 22 June, after having been confined during the interval in the Black Hole of Sheerness garrison. Ten officers, under the presidency of Vice-Admiral Sir Thomas Pasley, Bart., composed the court-martial, which sat on board the *Neptune,* off Greenhithe. The prisoner conducted his own defence, exhibiting great presence of mind, and preserving a respectful and manly deference throughout towards his judges.

The prosecution on the part of the Crown lasted two days, and on the 26th, Parker called witnesses in his favour, and read a long and able defence which he had previously prepared. The line of argument adopted by him was – that the situation he had held had been in a measure forced upon him; that he had consented to assume it chiefly from the hope of restraining the men from excesses; that he had restrained them in various instances; that he might have taken all the ships to sea, or to an enemy's port, had his motives been disloyal, etc. Parker unquestionably spoke the truth on many of these points. Throughout the whole affair, the injury done to property was trifling, the taking of some flour from a vessel being the chief act of the kind. But he had indubitably been the head of the mutineers. It was proved that he went from ship to ship giving orders and encouraging the men to stand out, and that his orders were given as though he were actually admiral of the fleet. Nothing could save him. He was sentenced to death. When his doom was pronounced, he rose, and said, in firm tones, "I shall submit to your sentence with all due respect, being confident in the innocency of my intentions, and that God will receive me unto His favour; and I sincerely hope that my death will be the means of restoring tranquillity to the Navy, and that those men who have been implicated in the business may be reinstated in their former situations, and again be serviceable to their country."

On the morning of 30 June, the yellow flag, the signal of death, was hoisted on board the *Sandwich,* where Richard Parker lay, and where he was to meet his fate. The whole fleet was ranged a little below Sheerness, in sight of the *Sandwich,* and the crew of every ship was piped to the forecastle. Parker was awakened from a sound sleep on that morning, and after being shaved, he dressed himself in a suit of deep mourning. He mentioned to his attendants that he had made a will, leaving to his wife some property in Devonshire that belonged to him. On coming to the deck, he was pale, but perfectly composed, and drank a glass of wine "to the salvation of his soul, and forgiveness of all his enemies!" He said nothing to his mates on the forecastle but "Good-bye to you!" and expressed a hope that "his death would be deemed sufficient atonement, and save the lives of others."

He was strung up to the yard-arm at half-past nine o'clock. A dead silence reigned among the crews around during the execution. When cold, his body was taken down, put in a shell [coffin], and interred within an hour or two after his death in the new naval burying ground at Sheerness.

Richard Parker's unfortunate wife had not left Scotland when the news reached her ears that the Nore fleet had mutinied, and that the ringleader was one Richard Parker. She could not doubt that this was her husband, and immediately took a place in the mail for London, to save him if possible. On her arrival, she heard that Parker had been tried, but the result was not known. Being able to think of no way but petitioning the King, she gave a person a guinea to draw up a paper, praying that her husband's life might be spared. She attempted to make her way with this into His Majesty's presence, but was obliged finally to hand it to a lord-in-waiting, who gave her the cruel intelligence that all applications for mercy would be attended to, except for Parker.

The distracted woman then took coach for Rochester, where she got on board a King's ship, and learnt that Parker was to be executed next day. She sat up, in a condition of unspeakable wretchedness, the whole of that night, and at four o'clock in the morning went to the riverside to hire a boat to take her to the *Sandwich*, that she might at least bid her poor husband farewell.

Her feelings had been deeply wrung by hearing every person she met talking on the subject of her distress, and now the first waterman to whom she spoke refused to take her as a single passenger. "The brave Admiral Parker is to die today," he said, "and I can get any sum I choose to ask for carrying over a party."

Finally, the wretched wife was glad to go on board a Sheerness market boat, but no boat was allowed to run up alongside of the *Sandwich*. In her desperation she called on Parker by name, and prevailed on the boat people, moved by the sight of her distress, to attempt to approach, but they were stopped by a sentinel who threatened to fire at them, unless they withdrew.

As the hour drew nigh, she saw her husband appear on deck walking between two clergymen. She called to him, and he heard her voice, for he exclaimed, "There is my dear wife from Scotland."

Then, happily, she fainted, and did not recover till some time after she was taken ashore. By this time all was over, but the poor woman could not believe it so. She hired another boat, and again reached the *Sandwich*. Her exclamation from the boat must have startled all who heard it. "Pass the word," she cried in her delusion, "for Richard Parker!"

On reaching the *Sandwich* she was informed that all was over and that the body of her husband had just been taken ashore for burial. She immediately caused herself to be rowed ashore again, but found the ceremony was over and the cemetery gate was locked. Excited almost to madness by the information given her that probably the surgeons would disinter the body that night and cut it up, she waited around the churchyard till dusk, and then clambering over the wall readily found her husband's grave. The shell was not buried deep, and she was not long in scraping away the loose earth. She tore off the lid with her nails and teeth, and then clasped the hand of her husband, cold in death and no more able to return the pressure.

Her determination to possess the body next forced her to seek the assistance of several men to undertake the lifting of the body. This was accomplished successfully, and at 3 a.m. the shell containing the corpse was placed in a van and conveyed to Rochester, where, for the sum of six guineas, the widow procured another wagon to carry it to London.

At 11 p.m. the van reached London, but there the poor widow had no private house or friends to go to, and was constrained to stop at the "Hoofs and Horseshoe" on Tower Hill, which was full of people. Mrs Parker got the body into her room, and sat down beside it; but the secret could not long be kept in such a place, more particularly as the news of the exhumation had been brought by express that day to London.

An immense crowd assembled about the house, anxious to see the body of Parker, but this the widow would not permit.

The Lord Mayor heard of the affair, and came to ask the widow what she intended to do with her husband's remains. She replied, "To inter them decently at Exeter or in Scotland." The Lord Mayor assured her that the body would not be taken from her, and eventually prevailed on her to consent to its being decently buried in London. Arrangements were made with this view, and in the interim it was taken to Aldgate Workhouse, on account of the crowds attracted by it, which caused some fears "lest Admiral Parker's remains should provoke a civil war."

Finally, the corpse was buried in Whitechapel Churchyard, and Mrs Parker, who had in person seen her husband consigned to the grave, gave a certificate that all had been done to her satisfaction. But, though strictly questioned as to her accomplices in the exhuming and carrying away of the body, she firmly refused to disclose the names.

Richard Parker was a remarkably fine man. The brilliancy and expression of his eyes were of such a nature as caused one of the witnesses at his trial, while under examination, to break down, and quail beneath his glance, and shrink abashed, incapacitated from giving further testimony.